Hello There, you are about to partake on a wonderous journey of art originally conceived as Star Wars characters some of these villains and heroes became part of a new genera called the Galaxy Wars, as you see each picture you will see where the concepts came from and I will explain each picture as well. Plus I will tell you about their species.

Come with me, and enter the Realm of Galaxy Wars.

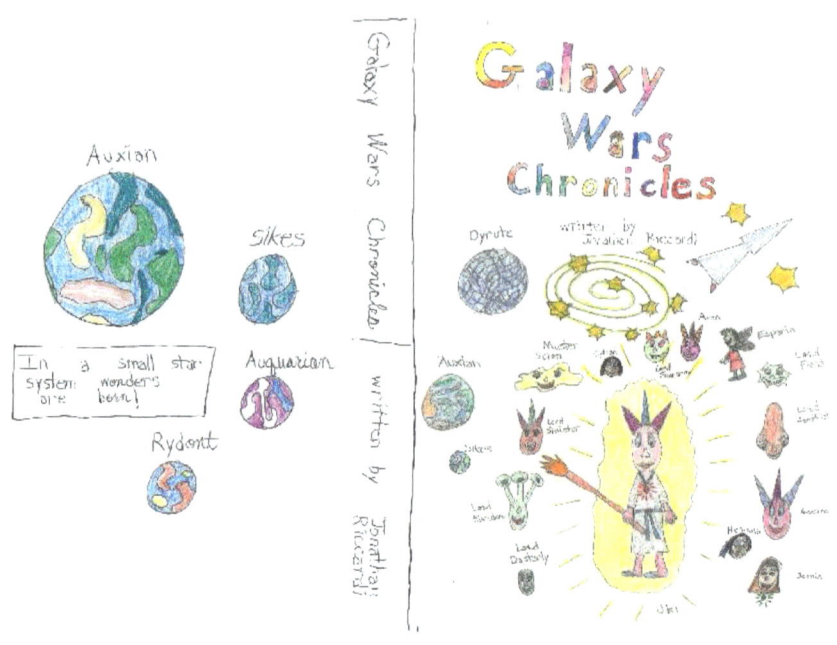

This image here represents the cover of the book the final concept of the first book is on the right. The next Volume contains the left.

Darth Avonica

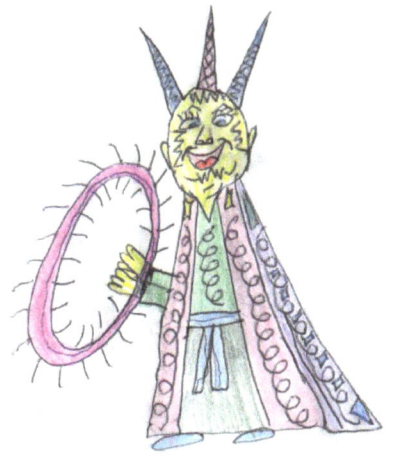

Ep 6½ 6¾

species : Flores

This is an image of Princess Avonica before she was changed into a hero, she is very important to the Galaxy Wars story in that she defeats her evil brother and raises her daughter who turns out to be very special indeed.

This may be the original drawling too. I'm not sure.

She comes from the planet of Auxian where every four hours the moon of Sikes rotates. Her character is very gentle and kind but also she can fight with the best of them, as she learns more from her master Shion there is no limit to her wisdom.

Her species is considered among the finest chefs and once or twice a local patron tells of the fine cooked Gorsh that live among the plains of Auxian.

Perhaps the most respected Auxian of all is the one called Uki, Uki fought in the Collaterial Wars and saved the Galaxy from trouble, although trapped by temptation of total power her friend Nova whom she discovered on her journey saved her.

The Galaxy is forever in their debt.

Darth Monaor

species
Serpulus

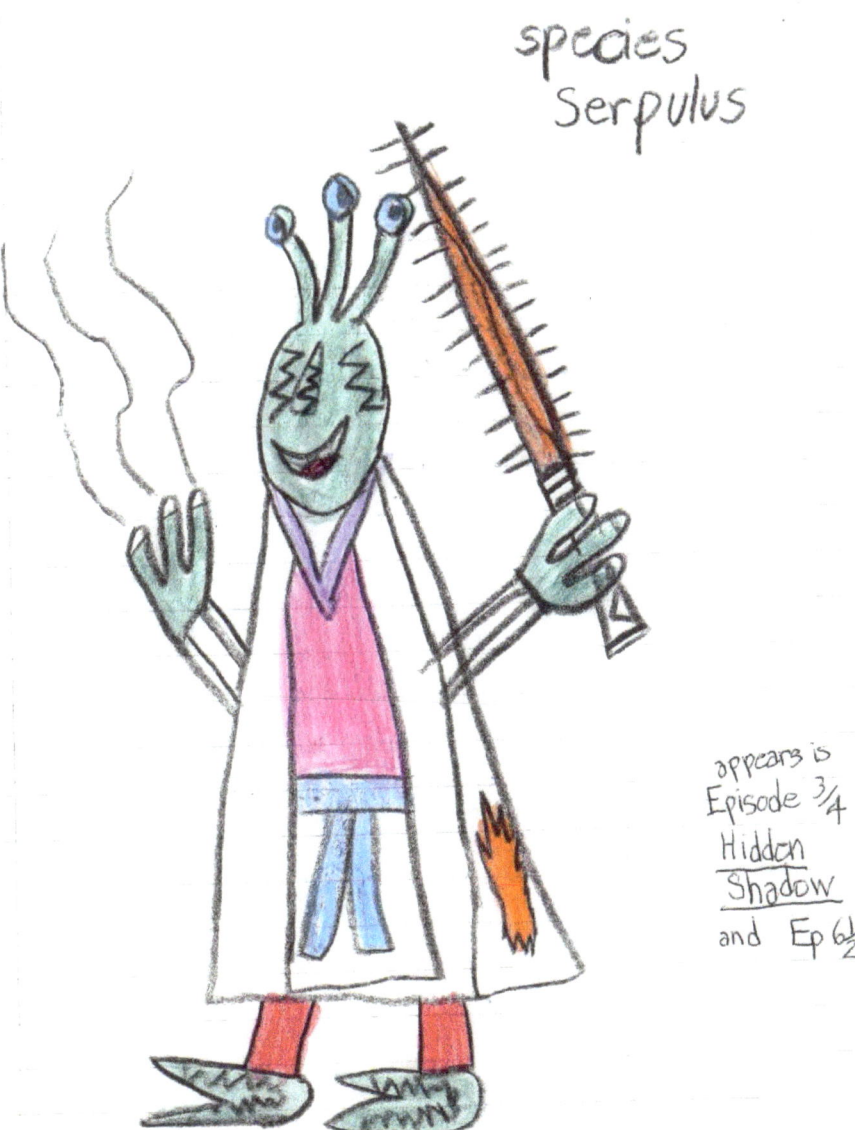

appears is
Episode 3/4
Hidden
Shadow
and Ep 6½

As you can see the original idea of the character was to be evil and well that idea stayed, his name also stayed the same.

He is a main antagonist for our heroes.

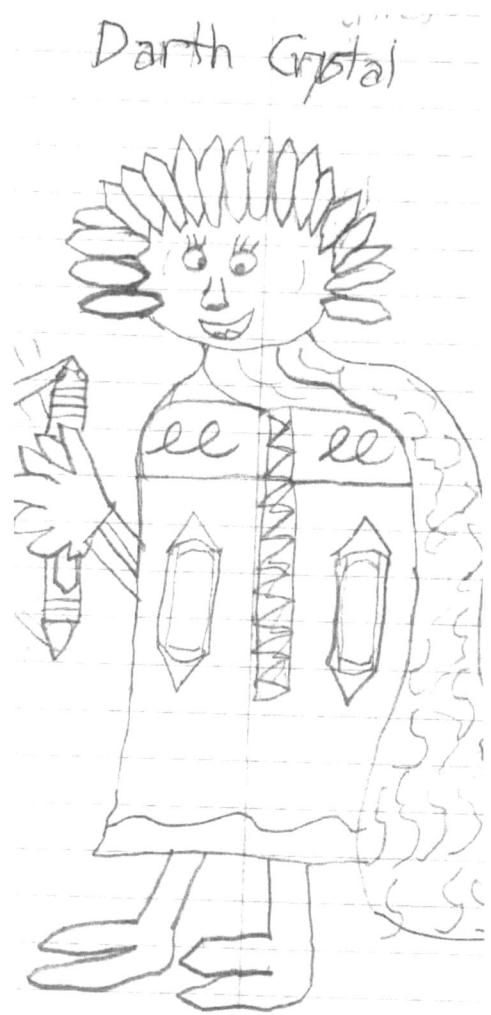

Darth Crystal

Another Cute character of the Realm is Lord Crystal
She was conceived then finally used in one of the
stories, I believe her true fate is yet to be known.

She may yet return to either plague or help our heroes.

Her favorite pastimes are admiring her good looks.

Darth Renderous

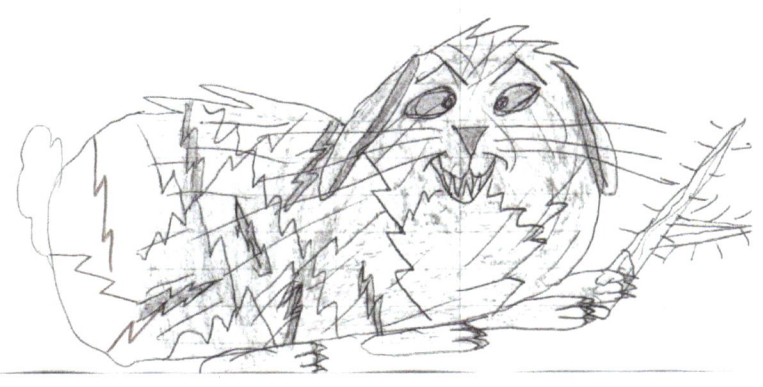

→ Darth Echo

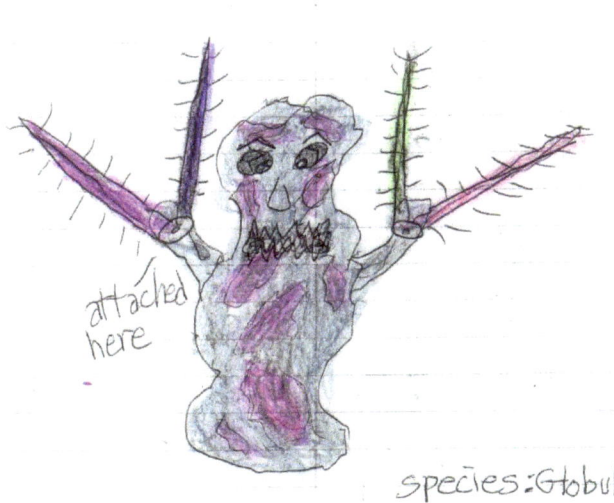

attached here

species: Globul

The character on the bottom was used in book 2 and he loves and craves power, he was made to look ugly and pure evil, also he was created originally as a major villain and he stayed true to that.

Darth Tyrune

Ep 6¾

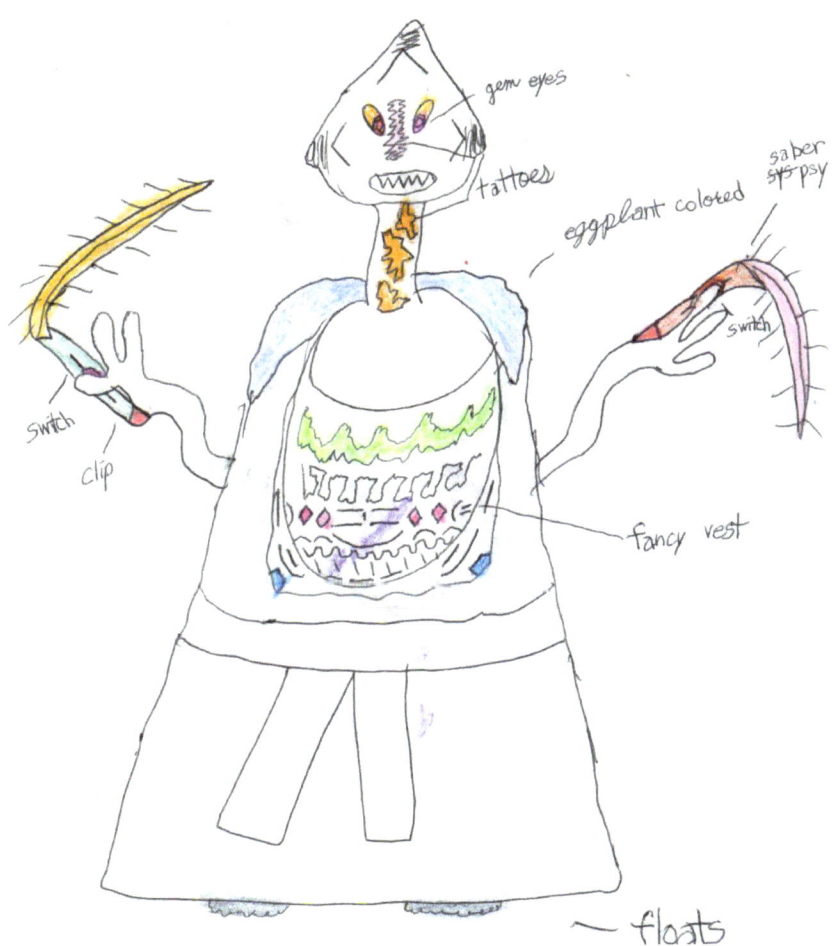

gem eyes

tattoes

saber sys·psy

eggplant colored

switch

clip

switch

fancy vest

~ floats

This character made it into the last volume as a sacrifice to destroy the hero, but the Chosen One won't go down without a fight.

Darth Fiend

black and deadly

species: leafite

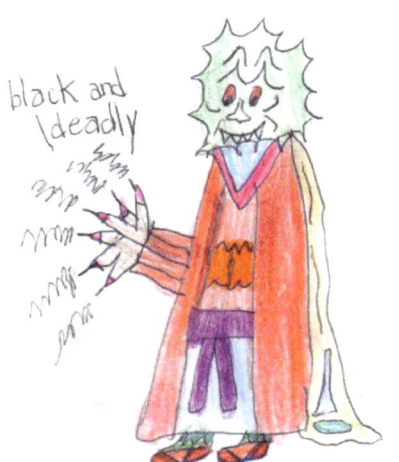

This guy is a frightful mess, when not conquering Galaxies he is seen using his powers for evil purposes.

Darth Lunie

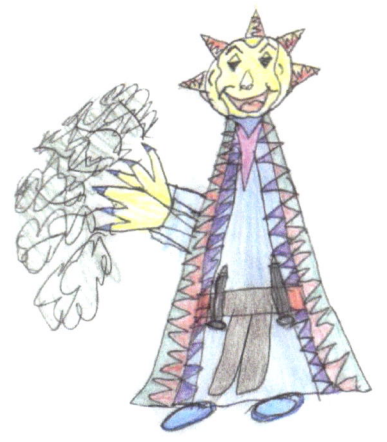

Ep $6\frac{1}{2}$ $6\frac{3}{4}$

species : Stromite

This sunny character is actually more focused on consuming power than it seems, although not evil he obeys any command given to him by his superiors.

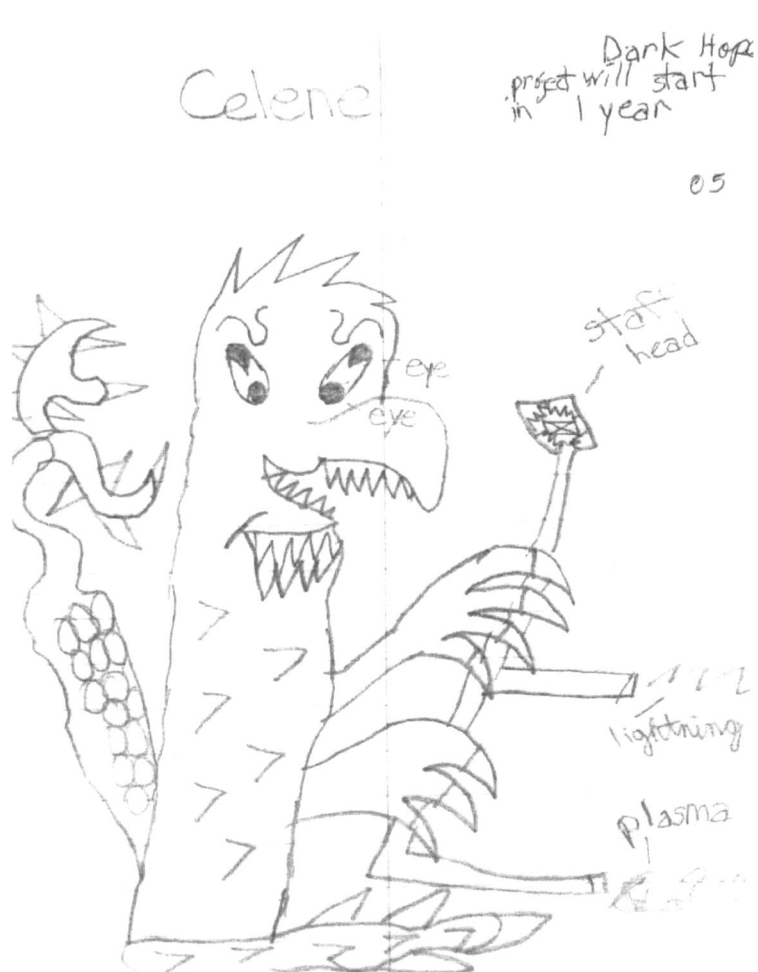

This evil creature resides on a distant planet where it's chilly and warm at the same time.

The only loyalty you will find with a Celene is who's got a higher bid.

Stay clear of this dude.

Darth Quesy

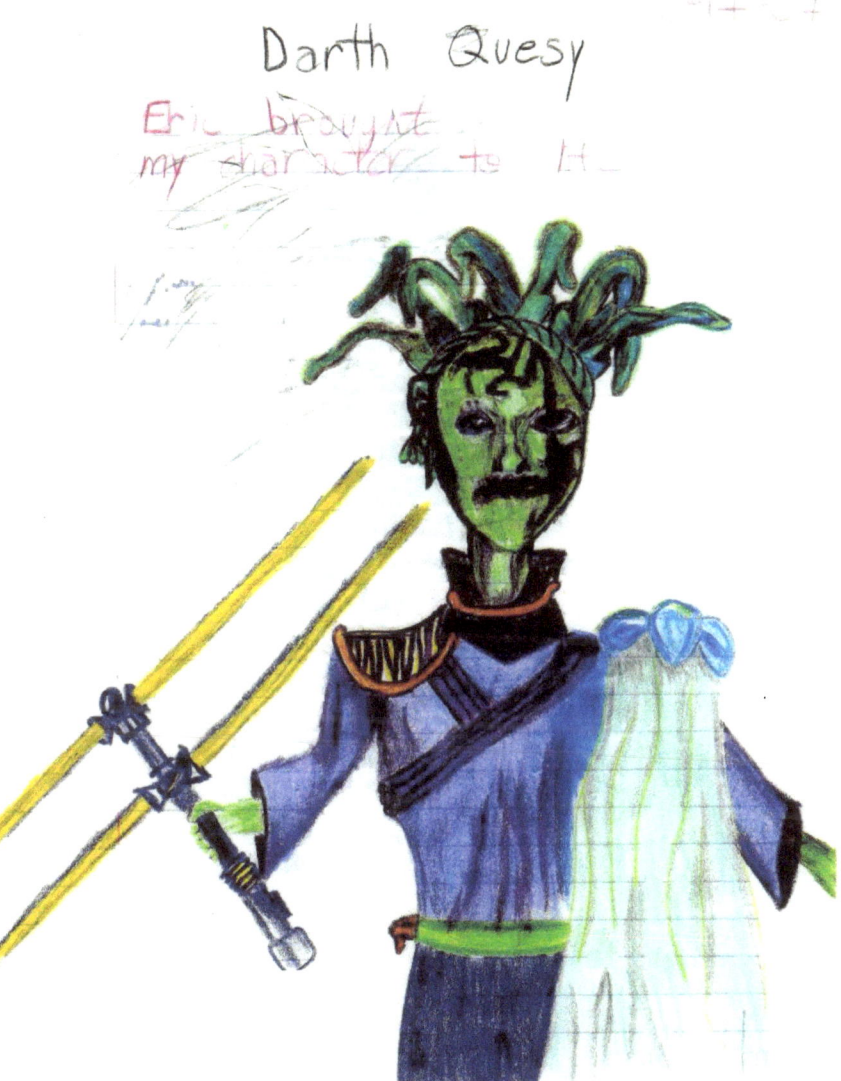

I do not remember who drew this evil character but she also appears in the story, she is merciless and filled with guile, repugnant in fact, if you do business with her stand back!

Darth Flora

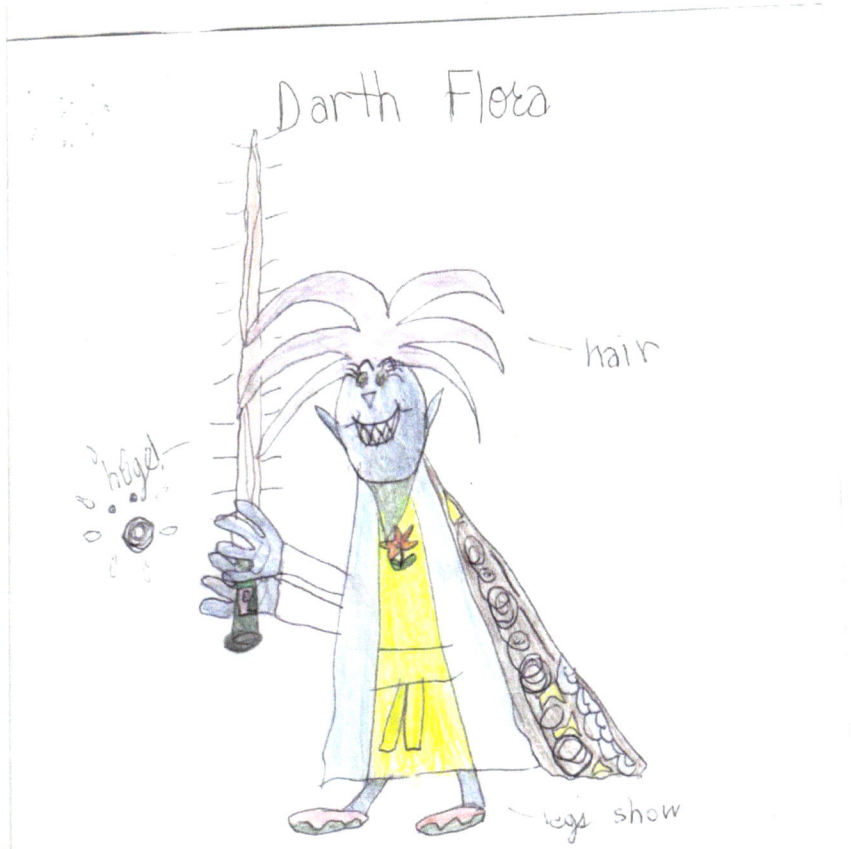

hair

h&ye!

species: Grinka

This concept is not yet produced but she is a popular drawling so here she is.

She will probably appear as a new villain in books 3 through 6.

Pedestrid   DK Jedi

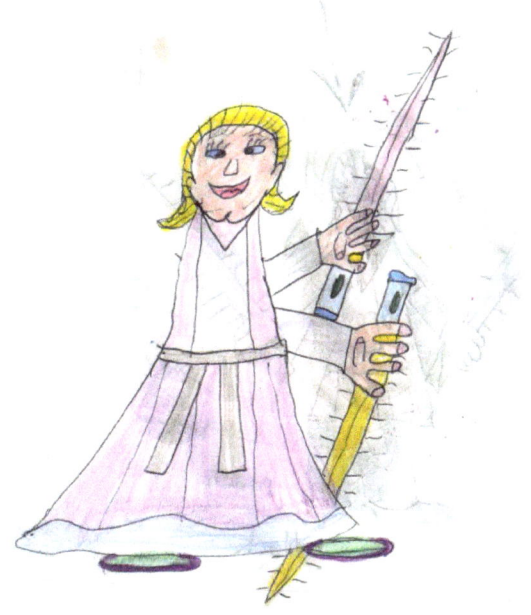

Ep 3/4 6½ 6¾

Prettier than her older sister Shatheed this lady is prepared to fight the villains with all she's got and that includes her looks too.

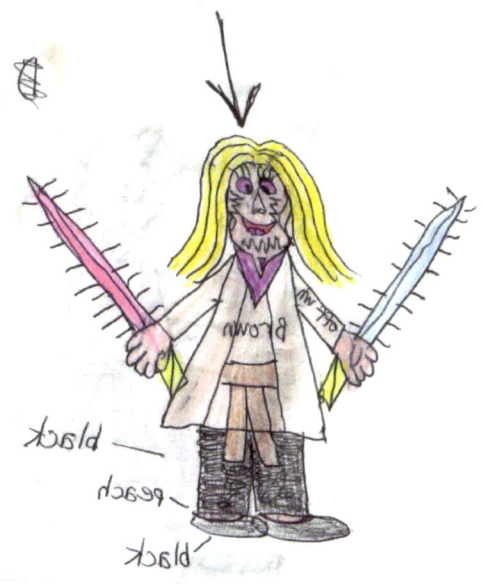

Shatheed is not as cute as her sister but packs a punch watch out if you encounter her.

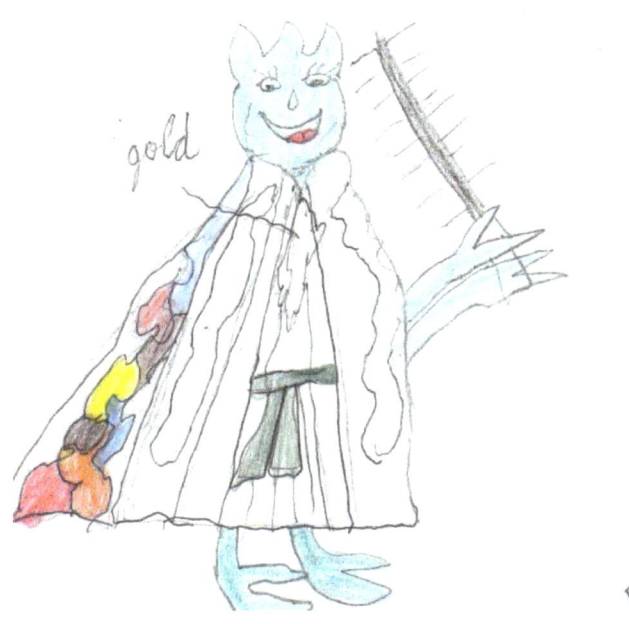

Darth Vidor

gold

Ep 6¾

This cute female creature cares more for her looks then fighting, she usually strives for more peaceful means.

Darth Rosebush

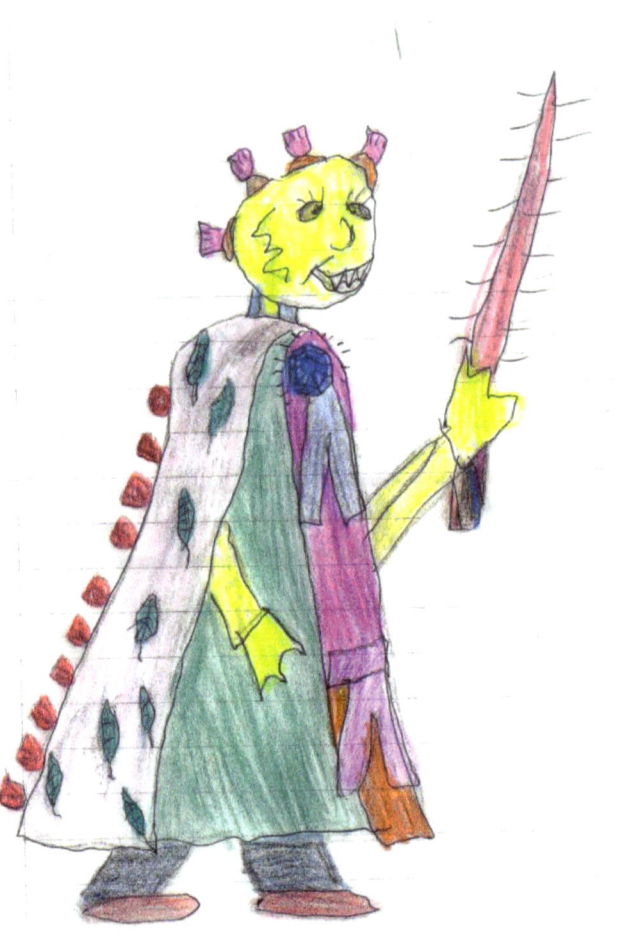

Ep. 6½
+ 6¾

Ruthless and merciless this bad momma will turn you inside out, she cares more for her looks then life itself. Watch out she's coming!

3-14-05

Dark Hope

Darth Mystical

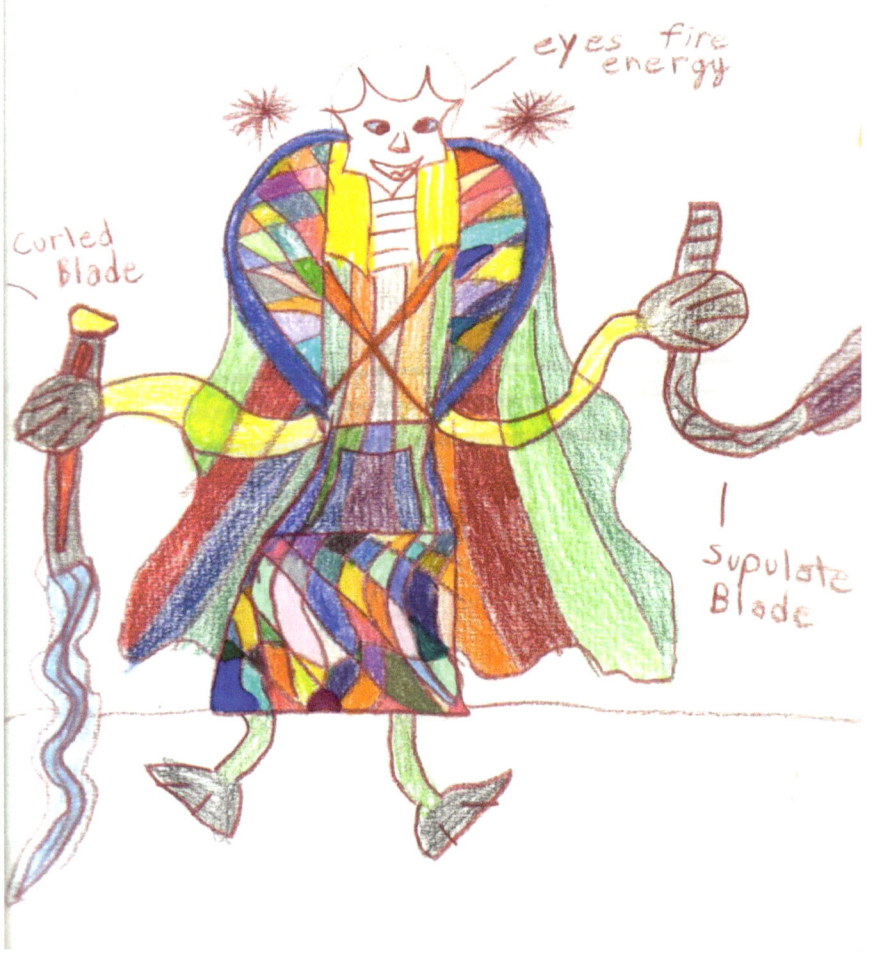

eyes fire energy

Curled Blade

supulate Blade

This villain loves nothing more than using his magical powers on the unsuspecting.

Master
Scion

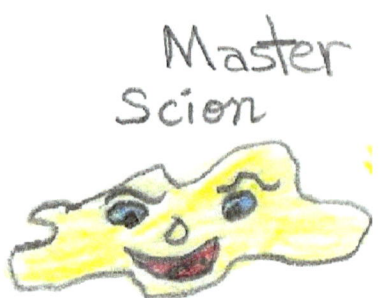

With his good looks and amazing speed Master
Scion is a match for even the most cunning of
villains, that combined with his magical skill at
Ganra make him a formidable opponent.

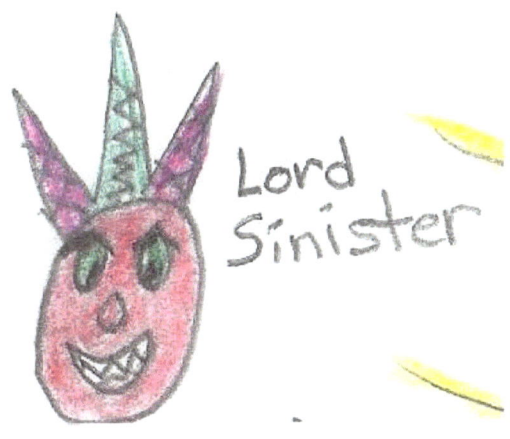

Lord
Sinister

This
was once Avonica's beloved brother, now twisted
and corrupted this monsterous enemy tests Avonica
to the core.

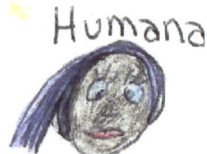

Humana

This brave hero starts as an innocent Congresswoman to become The Sub Head of the Rebellian of Worlds.

She likes to plan out meals with a pot of Lacrobian Coffee.

This little friend comes in a large package friendly and fashionable, talkative and cheery Esparia is a good conversationalist if you have the time.

Who doesn't in a chaotic galaxy.

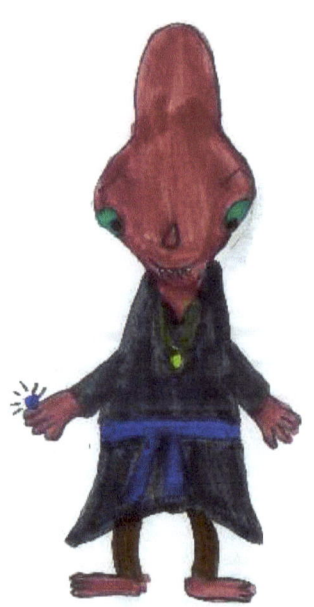

Once a follower of the bad side now looks at little

Uki with care and concern, as he breathes his last breath it will be a concerning day for all.

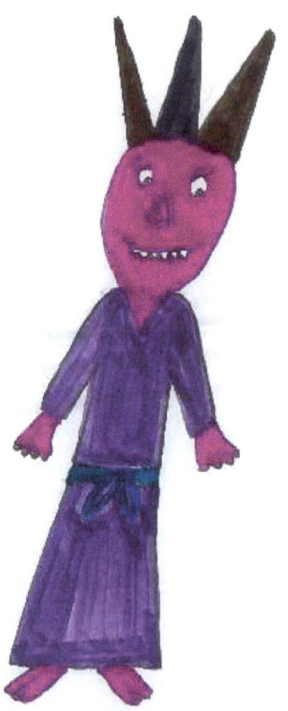

This fashionable motesta is playing both sides of the board unfortunately for her she is lured more and more to the bad side without really a hint of understanding.

She eventually winds up dead then reawakened for a vengeance.

Cylean

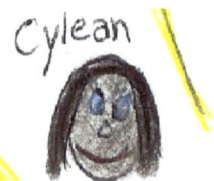

Friend Of Yurbal Glash this feminine hero stands for freedom even when faced with great strife and perdictaments, do not underestimate her that's for sure.

Wife of Yurbal Glash she soon finds her loyalty compromised as an Empire builds around her.

Lord
Dasterly

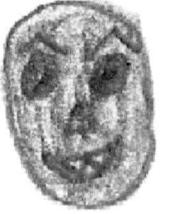

Evil knows no bounds as Yurbal Glash is consumed by darkness he becomes the Dark Lord Dasterly one of the most ruthless villains ever! Ruler of a new Empire this villain strikes hard at a fragile system of planets revolving around Auxian.

'Auxian

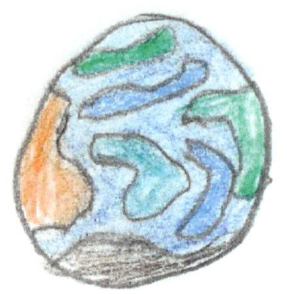

Sikes

Twin bodies that circle each other, no system is more important in it's own history then the Auxian System.

This lush world is home to the Chosen Ones two amazing females of extrodanary talent.

Be sure to stop at it's nearby moon Aquarian, it's beauty is unmatched in the galaxy!

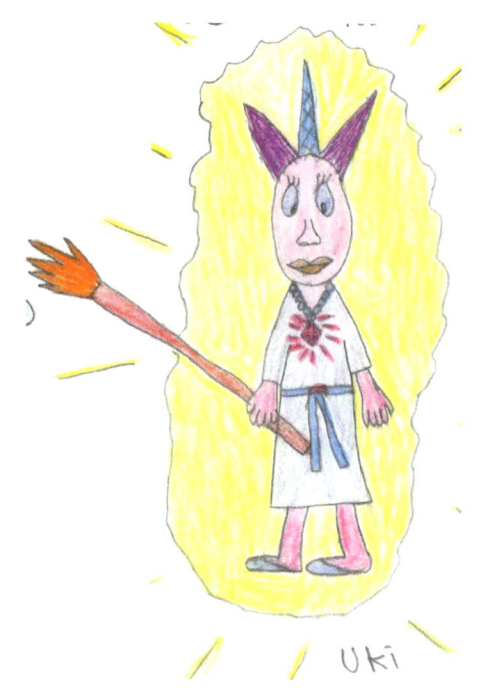

This amazing lady is also the most special, she balances the galaxy out by avoiding the dark and becoming a guardian of peace, this almost didn't happen though it took an old mage named Nova to bring it forth.

Thanks to their efforts the Galaxy is once more ready to prosper.

Well that's it I hoped you enjoyed this romp through the valley of the unexplored, well anyway it was unexplored.

I don't know if I will produce any more books after this one, but who knows. Plans are in the works for a second Galaxy Wars Trilogy.

Jonathan